Reading/Writing Companion

McGraw Hill

mheducation.com/prek-12

Send all inquiries to:
McGraw Hill
1325 Avenue of the Americas
New York, NY 10019

ISBN: 978-1-26-574008-5
MHID: 1-26-574008-9

Printed in the United States of America.

5 6 7 8 9 LMN 26 25 24 23 22

A

Welcome to WONDERS!

We are so excited about how much you will learn and grow this year! We're here to help you set goals for your learning.

You will build on what you already know and learn new things every day.

You will read a lot of fun stories and interesting texts on different topics.

You will write about the texts you read. You will also write texts of your own. You will do research as well.

You will explore new ideas by reading different texts.

Each week, we will set goals on the My Goals page. Here is an example:

I can read and understand texts.

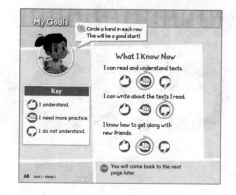

I need more practice with reading and understanding texts. I'll circle the **sideways thumb**.

I'm just learning how to read and understand texts. I'll circle **thumbs down** for now.

I can read and understand texts. I'll circle **thumbs up**.

As you read and write, you will learn skills and strategies to help you reach your goals.

You will think about your learning and sometimes circle a hand to show your progress.

Here are some questions you can ask yourself.

- Did I understand the task?
- Was it easy?
- Was it hard?
- What made it hard?

It is okay if I need more practice. The most important thing is to do my best and keep learning!

If you need more help, you can choose what to do.

- Talk to a friend or teacher.
- Use an Anchor Chart.
- Choose a center activity.

At the end of each week, you will complete a fun task to show what you have learned.

Then you will return to your My Goals page and think about your learning.

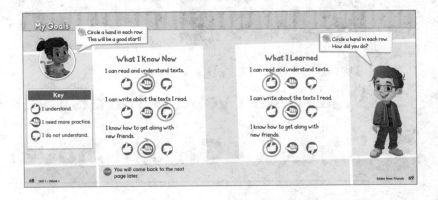

Unit 8 From Here to There

The Big Idea

Week 1 • On the Move

Week 2 • My U.S.A.

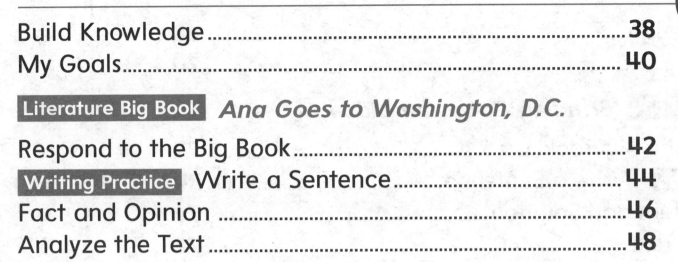

Week 3 • Look to the Sky

Extended Writing

Fantasy

Connect and Reflect

Oleg Shishkov/Shutterstock

From Here to There

The Big Idea

Where can you go that is near and far?

 Talk about places that are near the children.

 Circle places that are far away that you would like to visit.

Build Knowledge

? Essential Question **What can help you go from here to there?**

Build Vocabulary

 Talk about what can help you go to different places. What are some words that name what can help you go to different places?

 Draw a picture of one of the words.

 Write the word.

Daniel MacDonald/Flickr/Getty Images

My Goals

 Circle a hand in each row.
Everyone learns more with practice.

What I Know Now

I can read and understand texts.

I can write about the texts I read.

I know what can help me go from here to there.

Key

 I understand.

 I need more practice.

 I do not understand.

 You will come back to the next page later.

Circle a hand in each row.
What helped you the most?

What I Learned

I can read and understand texts.

I can write about the texts I read.

I know what can help me go from here to there.

Retell the realistic fiction story.

 Write about the story.

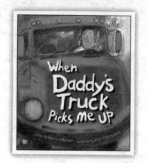

What is an interesting part of the story?

_____

- -

_____

How do you know this story is realistic fiction?

_____

- -

_____

- -

_____

Text Evidence

Page

Text Evidence

Page

Talk about how the boy feels while waiting for his daddy.

 Write about a time you waited for something fun. How did you feel?

I waited for

_____

- -

_____

I felt

_____

- -

_____

Writing Practice

Write a Sentence

 Talk about Daddy's long trip in the story.

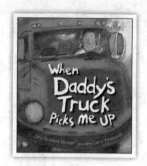

 Listen to this sentence about taking a trip.

We took a train to visit my grandpa.

Circle the end mark in the sentence.

Writing Skill

Remember: An **end mark**, such as a period, tells the end of a sentence.

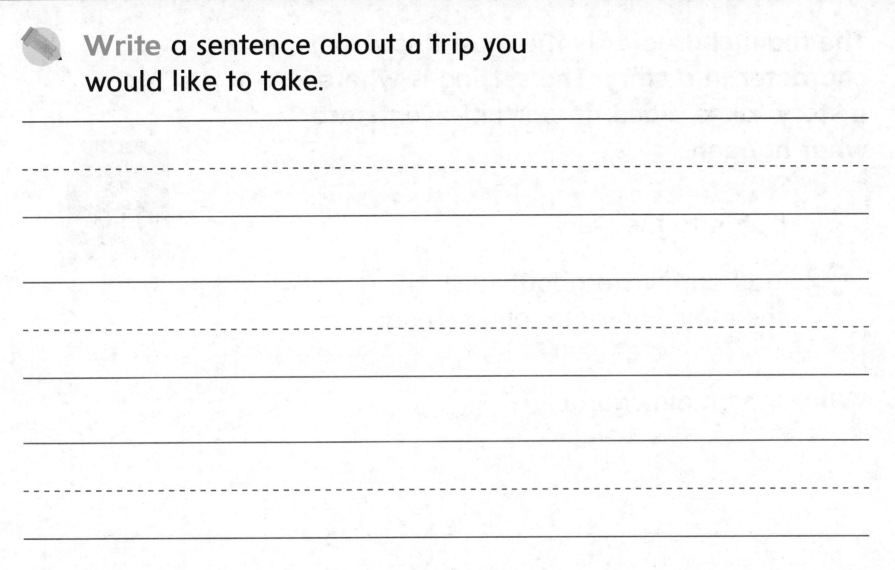

Write a sentence about a trip you would like to take.

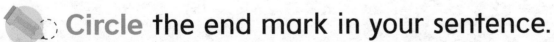 **Circle** the end mark in your sentence.

The **main character** is the most important character in a story. The **setting** is where a story takes place. **Important events** are what happen.

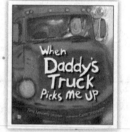

 Listen to the story.

 Talk and **write** about the main character and setting.

Who is the main character?

_____

- -

_____

Describe the setting.

_____

- -

_____

Talk and **write** about important events.

Beginning

Middle

End

Listen to and **look** at page 5.

 Talk about how the words tell that the boy is excited to see his daddy. How does the picture show this?

 Write about the words and picture.

Which words tell how the boy feels?

_____

- -

_____

What does the picture show?

_____

- -

_____

Look at page 14. How does the author show the words on this page?

 Talk about why the author shows the words in this way.

 Draw and **write** about it.

Find Text Evidence

 Make a prediction about the story. Use the title and pictures to help you. Read to find out if your prediction is correct.

 Read page 21. Point to each word in each sentence as you read.

Dad Got a Job

Dad got a job at a dock.

We had to pack up.

🔍 **Find Text Evidence**

✏️ **Underline** the uppercase letters in each sentence on page 22.

✏️ **Circle** a word that begins with the same sounds as **queen**.

"Pack with me," Dad said.

We can set up a big box.

I pack my red hat.

Tug! Tug! Lug! Lug!

"Jam it in," said Dad.

I quit on box six!

Find Text Evidence

Think about what has happened so far in the story. Make a prediction about what will happen next.

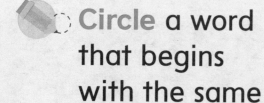 **Circle** a word that begins with the same sound as **jump**.

A big box can fit in a van!

We did it! We did it!

We had to get on a bus.

A quick bus got us to a jet.

Shared Read

 **Find Text Evidence**

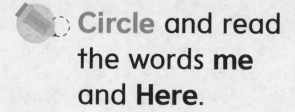 **Circle** and read the words **me** and **Here**.

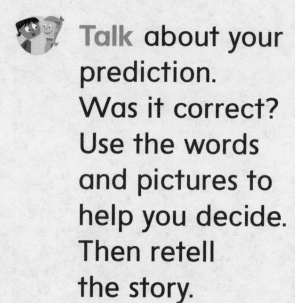 **Talk** about your prediction. Was it correct? Use the words and pictures to help you decide. Then retell the story.

We got on a quick jet!

Jack did not sit with me.

Jack had to sit in a bin.

We got in a tan cab.

Here is the dock!

"Not bad, Dad!" I said.

Shania

Write About the Shared Read

Dad Got a Job

How does the girl get to the dock with her dad and Jack?

 Look at what Shania drew.

 Listen to what she wrote.

Grammar

Prepositions tell about nouns. The words *in, on, up,* and *with* are prepositions.

First, they take a bus to a jet. But Jack cannot sit with them. He stays in a cage. Then they ride in a cab to the dock. They see a big ship there!

Talk about the sentences Shania wrote. What do you notice?

Underline a preposition in the third sentence.

Circle an end mark in the last sentence.

Writing Trait

Remember:
A sentence tells a complete idea.

Write About the Shared Read

How do the girl and her dad get ready to move?

 Talk about the question.

 Draw your ideas.

Write about your ideas.
Use your drawing to help you.

_____

- -

_____

- -

_____

_____

- -

_____

- -

Remember:

☐ Write complete sentences.

☐ Use prepositions.

☐ Add an end mark to each sentence.

Check In 👍 ✊ 👎

Look at the painting of the people riding on the stagecoach.

 Talk about how it shows people and things from long ago.

SuperStock/Getty Images

Quick Tip

You can use these sentence starters:

Long ago, people used ____.

Long ago, there were ____.

Look at pages 33–36. What do the words in red tell you?

 Talk about why the author organized this text into "Long Ago" and "Today." What information do these titles tell?

 Write about it.

Talk About It

Compare how people traveled long ago and today. How has traveling changed?

What does the author tell about in "Long Ago?"

_____

- -

_____

What does the author tell about in "Today?"

_____

- -

_____

Kinds of Vehicles

Step 1 **Talk** about vehicles people use on the land, in the water, and in the air. Choose one to learn about.

Step 2 **Write** a question about how this vehicle moves from one place to another.

_____

- -

_____

_____

_____

Step 3 **Look** at books or use the Internet. Look up words you do not know. Use a picture or online dictionary.

Step 4 Draw what you learned. Add labels.

Step 5 Write about what you learned in your writer's notebook. Use new words that you learned.

Step 6 Choose a good way to present your work.

Talk about these trains.
Which train is from long ago?
Which train is from today?
How do you know?

 Compare these trains to the truck
in *When Daddy's Truck Picks Me Up.*

Quick Tip

You can use these
sentence starters:

*The black train
is from ____.*

*The white train
is from ____.*

Write About a Vehicle

① **Think** about the texts you read. What did you learn about what can help you go to places near and far?

② **Choose** a place to visit. What vehicle would you use to go to this place? **Draw** the vehicle.

③ **Write** about why you would use this vehicle. Use words that you learned this week.

Think about what you learned this week. Turn to page 11.

Build Knowledge

Build Vocabulary

 Talk about what you know about our country. What are some words that name what you know about our country?

 Draw a picture of one of the words.

Write the word.

MATTES RenÄ©/hemis.fr/Getty Images

My Goals

 Circle a hand in each row.
It is important to keep learning.

What I Know Now

I can read and understand texts.

I can write about the texts I read.

I know about our country.

Key

 I understand.

 I need more practice.

 I do not understand.

 You will come back to the next page later.

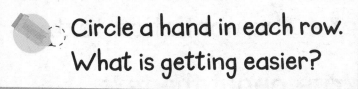

Circle a hand in each row. What is getting easier?

What I Learned

I can read and understand texts.

I can write about the texts I read.

I know about our country.

Retell the nonfiction text.

 Write about the text.

What is one fact that Ana learns?

 Text Evidence

Page

What is something interesting that you learned?

Text Evidence

Page

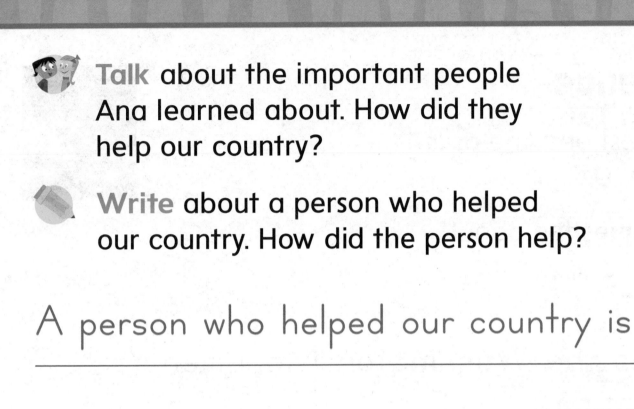 **Talk** about the important people Ana learned about. How did they help our country?

Write about a person who helped our country. How did the person help?

A person who helped our country is

This person helped

Write a Sentence

 Talk about questions Ana asks in Washington, D.C.

 Listen to this question about Washington, D.C.

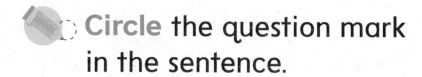

How tall is the Washington Monument?

Circle the question mark in the sentence.

Writing Skill

A **question mark** is one kind of end mark. It tells that someone is asking a question.

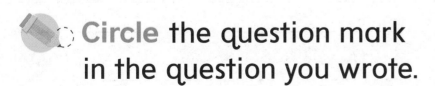**Write** a question you have about Washington, D.C.

_____

- - - - - - - - - - - - - - - - - -

_____

- - - - - - - - - - - - - - - - - -

_____

- - - - - - - - - - - - - - - - - -

_____

- - - - - - - - - - - - - - - - - -

_____

Circle the question mark in the question you wrote.

A fact in a text is information about a topic that can be proven true or false. An opinion is something a person feels or thinks about a topic.

 Listen to pages 20-21.

 Talk about the facts and opinions.

 Write one fact and one opinion.

What is one fact?

_____

- - - - - - - - - - - - - - - - - - -

_____

_____

- - - - - - - - - - - - - - - - - - -

_____

What is one opinion?

_____

- -

_____

_____

- -

_____

 Talk about which words help you spot an opinion. Explain.

Check In

Look at page 6.

 Talk about why the illustrator put photos on the map.

Circle **yes** or **no** to each question about the photos.

1. Do they show real places?   **yes**   **no**

2. Do they show what the places look like?   **yes**   **no**

3. Do they show where Ana lives?   **yes**   **no**

4. Do they show where Ana is?   **yes**   **no**

Listen to and **look** at pages 16–17.

 Talk about what is real on these pages.
What is make-believe?

 Draw in the boxes.

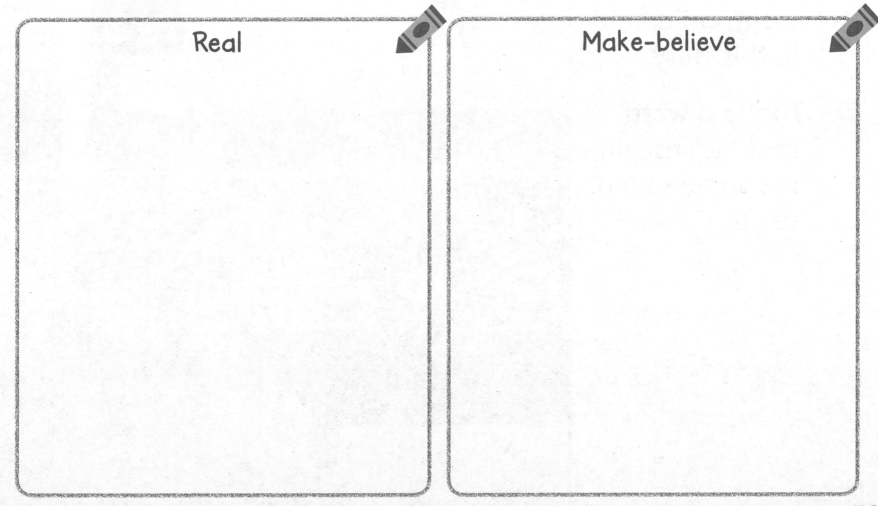

Real

Make-believe

Find Text Evidence

 Read the title. Look at the picture. Think about what you want to find out in this story.

Circle a word that begins with the same sound as **yam**.

Pack a Bag!

"Pop is here," said Zeb.

"Can I pack a big bag?"

Mom and Dad said, "Yes."

Shared Read

🔍 **Find Text Evidence**

✏️ ◯ **Circle** words that begin with the same sound as **zipper**.

✏️ ‥ **Underline** and read the word **What**.

Zeb can get on a big jet.

He can zip to Pop.

Zeb is not sad!

What can Zeb see?

Zeb can nod at a man.

Zeb can see a big, big sun.

Shared Read

Find Text Evidence

Underline and read the word **this.**

Circle who can go up, up, up. Then say a sentence that tells who goes up.

It was a quick, quick jet!

Zeb and Pop hug.

Pop got this pack for Zeb.

Pop and Zeb get up at six.

Pop can go up, up, up.

Zeb can go up, up, up.

Shared Read

Find Text Evidence

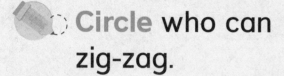

Circle who can zig-zag.

Retell the story. Reread if you do not understand something.

Pop can zig-zag.

Zeb is hot and not quick.

"Do not quit yet!" said Pop.

Yes! They get to the top.

Zeb did it. Pop did it.

Zeb can sit and sip.

Write About the Shared Read

Pack a Bag!

What do Zeb and Pop do together?

Maddie

 Look at what Maddie drew.

 Listen to what she wrote.

Grammar

Remember: A **preposition** tells about a noun in a sentence.

Denis Kuvaev/Shutterstock

Zeb and Pop hike up a mountain. Pop goes fast. Zeb is slow. When they get to the top, Pop is happy. Why is Zeb happy? He gets to rest!

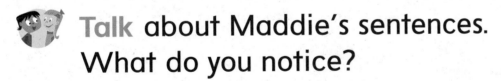 **Talk** about Maddie's sentences. What do you notice?

Underline a preposition in the first sentence.

Circle the question mark.

Writing Trait

Write long and short sentences to make your writing more interesting.

Write About the Shared Read

How do you know that Zeb enjoys his trip?

Pack a Bag!

 Talk about the question.

 Draw your ideas.

Write about your ideas.
Use your drawing to help you.

_____

- -

_____

- -

_____

- -

_____

- -

Remember:

☐ Write long and short sentences.

☐ Add a preposition.

☐ Use a question mark.

Check In

Look at the photos. What clues do they give about Ancestral Puebloan homes?

The Ancestral Puebloans were excellent builders. They made buildings several stories high with hundreds of rooms.

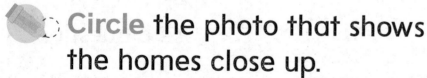 **Circle** the photo that shows the homes close up.

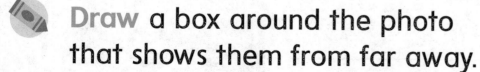 **Draw** a box around the photo that shows them from far away.

Quick Tip

You can say:

The close-up photo shows ___.

The faraway photo shows ___.

Talk and **write** about the photos and caption.

What did you learn from the close-up photo?

_____

- -

_____

What did you learn from the faraway photo?

_____

- -

_____

What did you learn from the caption?

_____

- -

_____

Talk About It

Why do you think the Ancestral Puebloans built homes in the cliffs?

An Important American

Step 1 **Talk** about Americans from long ago
who helped our country.
Choose one to learn about.

Step 2 **Write** a question about the person.

_____

- -

_____

_____

- -

_____

Step 3 **Look** at books or use the Internet.
Look up words you do not know.
Use a picture or online dictionary.

Step 4 Draw what you learned.

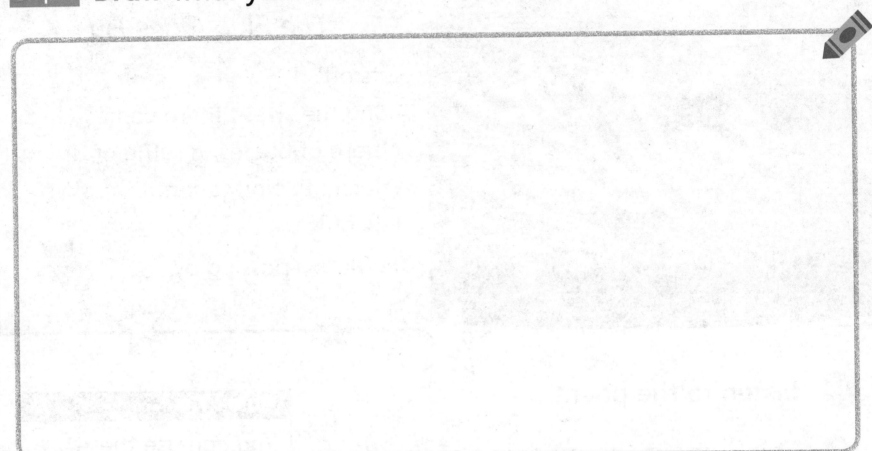

Step 5 Write about what you learned in your writer's notebook. Use new words that you learned.

Step 6 Choose a good way to present your work.

The Flag Goes By

Hats off!
Along the street there comes
A blare of bugles, a ruffle of drums,
A flash of color beneath the sky:
Hats off!
The flag is passing by.

Joseph De Sciose/Pixtal/AGE Fotostock; Bennett, Henry Holcomb. "The Flag Goes By." In *The Little Book of the Flag*, by Eva March Tappan, 98–99. Boston, New York, Chicago: Houghton Mifflin Company, 1917.

 Listen to the poem.

 Think about the meaning of the flag in the poem.

 Compare the flag in the poem to things Ana sees in Washington, D.C.

Quick Tip

You can use these sentence starters:

The flag in the poem ____.

Ana in the text sees ____.

Make a Travel Poster

① **Think** about the texts you read. What did you learn about places in our country?

② **Choose** a place that you learned about. **Draw** a poster that shows this place.

③ **Write** about why people should visit this place. Use words that you learned this week.

Think about what you learned this week.
Turn to page 41.

Build Knowledge

 Essential Question **What do you see in the sky?**

Build Vocabulary

 Talk about what you see in the sky. What are some words that name what you see in the sky?

 Draw a picture of one of the words.

 Write the word.

- -

My Goals

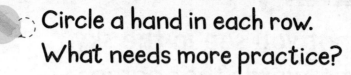
Circle a hand in each row.
What needs more practice?

Key

 I understand.

 I need more practice.

 I do not understand.

What I Know Now

I can read and understand texts.

I can write about the texts I read.

I know about what I see in the sky.

 You will come back to the next page later.

Circle a hand in each row. Great job!

What I Learned

I can read and understand texts.

I can write about the texts I read.

I know about what I see in the sky.

Retell the fantasy story.

 Write about the fantasy.

How do you know this story is a fantasy?

_____

- -

_____

 Text Evidence

Page

- -

_____

Why do you think Mole has not seen the moon before?

_____

Text Evidence

Page

- -

_____

Talk about how Mole thinks he can get the moon.

 Draw what you have imagined about the night sky.

Write a Sentence

 Talk about ways Mole tries to pull down the moon.

 Listen to this sentence about the moon.

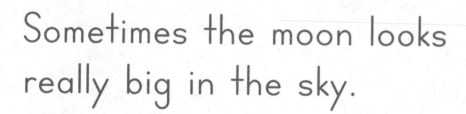

Sometimes the moon looks really big in the sky.

 Draw an arrow below the sentence from the first word to the last word.

Writing Skill

Remember:
When you write, the words go from left to right and top to bottom.

Write a sentence about the moon.
Turn a line when you write.

_____

- -

_____

- -

_____

- -

_____

Draw an arrow below your sentence
from the first word to the last word.

The **important events** in a story often have a **problem** and a **solution**.

- The **problem** is what a character wants to do or fix.

- The way the character solves the problem is the **solution**.

 Listen to the story.

 Talk and **write** about Mole's problem and how he tries to solve it.

Problem

Steps to Solution

Solution

Listen to and **look** at pages 18–19. What do the sound words "Oh! Eeek! Ouch! Ooh!" and SPLASH! tell you?

Draw and **write** about it.

The sound words tell

_____

- -

Listen to and **look** at pages 22–23.

 Talk and **write** about what happens on these pages.

What does Mole think happened to the moon?

_____

_____

What really happened?
How does the artist's picture help you to know?

_____

_____

_____

Find Text Evidence

Make a prediction about the text. Use the title and photos to help you. Read to find out if your prediction is correct.

Underline and read the words **have** and **here**.

Up! Up! Up!

I am Greg.

I have a fun job here.

I am in luck.

I can see up, up, up!

Shared Read

 Read from the top of the pages to the bottom, and from left to right. Point to each sentence as you read.

Circle what can dip and zip in the photo. Also circle the word.

This is what I can see.

A jet can dip.

It can zip up, up, up

on the trip!

Yes, a sun is big.

A sun can get hot.

I bet it can get up.

Find Text Evidence

 Think about what you have read so far. Make a prediction about what the rest of the text will be about.

 Circle the little cup that is up. Also circle the words **little cup**.

I can see a big cup.

I can see a little cup.

Yes, they are up!

AlexanderZam/Shutterstock

See up, up, up!

Is a dim dot on it?

Yes, it is a dot!

Find Text Evidence

 Circle words that begin with the same sounds as **quack**.

 Talk about your prediction. Was it correct? Use the words and photos to help you decide. Then retell the text.

It is a bit of rock and gas.

I want to see it zig-zag.

I can see it up, up, up!

StockTrek/Photodisc/Getty Images

I can see up, up, up.

It is a fun job for me.

I can not quit, quit, quit!

Ingram Publishing/SuperStock

Dimitri

Write About the Shared Read

Why does Greg say he is "in luck"?

 Look at what Dimitri drew.

 Listen to what he wrote.

Up! Up! Up!

Grammar

Remember: A **preposition** tells about a noun in a sentence.

Greg has a fun job! That is why he says he is lucky. He uses a telescope to see up in space. Greg can see dots on the moon up close. He also sees a bit of rock and gas. Greg wants to see it zig-zag!

 Talk about the sentences Dimitri wrote. What do you notice?

 Circle two prepositions in the third sentence.

 Draw an arrow below the second sentence from the first word to the last word.

Writing Trait

A sentence tells a complete idea. Every sentence has a noun and a verb.

Writing and Grammar

Write About the Shared Read

What does Greg learn while looking at the night sky?

 Talk about the question.

 Draw your ideas.

Write about your ideas.
Use your drawing to help you.

_____

- -

_____

- -

_____

_____

- -

_____

- -

_____

Remember:

☐ Write complete sentences.

☐ Use prepositions in sentences.

☐ Turn lines when you write.

Check In

Look at the photos of the day and night sky. How are day and night alike and different?

 Circle the parts that show it is day.

 Draw boxes around the parts that show it is night.

Quick Tip

You can use these sentence starters:

In the day, the sky is _____.

In the night, the sky is _____.

Look at the photo on page 30.

 Talk about why the author says the sun "looks like a giant fireball."

 Write about it.

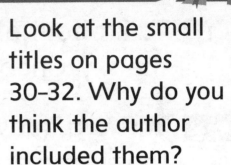
Talk About It

Look at the small titles on pages 30–32. Why do you think the author included them?

The sun and a giant fireball are both

_____

- -

_____

_____

- -

_____

_____

Objects in the Sky

Step 1 **Talk** about objects you can see in the sky. Choose one to learn about.

Step 2 **Write** a question about the sky object.

_____

- -

_____

- -

_____

Step 3 **Look** at books or use the Internet. Look up words you do not know. Use a picture or online dictionary.

Step 4 Draw what you learned.

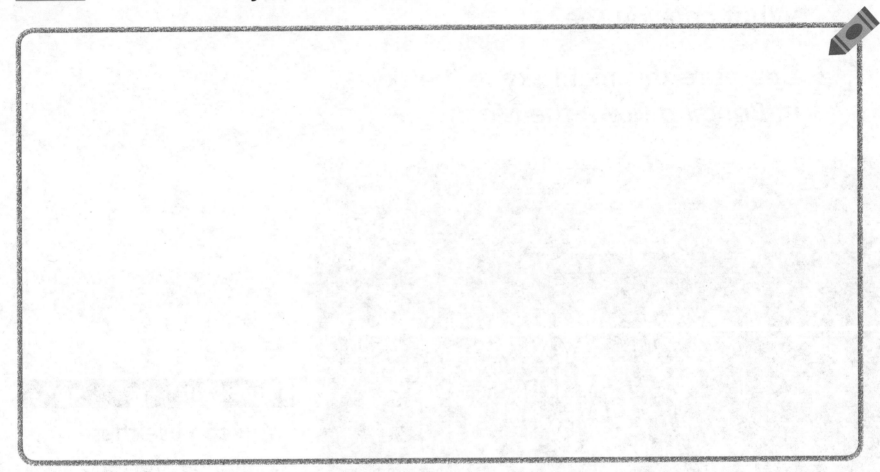

Step 5 Write about what you learned
in your writer's notebook.
Use new words that you learned.

Step 6 Choose a good way to present your work.

Talk about the night sky in the photo. What can you see?

 Compare this night sky to the sky in *Bringing Down the Moon.*

Fuse/Getty Images

Quick Tip

You can use these sentence starters:

The night sky in the photo is ____.

The night sky in the story is ____.

Write a Postcard

1 **Think** about the texts you read. What did you learn about things you can see in the sky?

2 **Pretend** you are in outer space. Send a postcard to a friend. **Draw** a picture of what you see on one side.

3 **Write** about what you see on the other side. Use words that you learned this week.

Think about what you learned this week. Turn to page 71.

Writing and Grammar

I wrote a fantasy story. My story has events that could not really happen.

Ellie

Fantasy
My fantasy story has animals that talk.

Student Model

Night-Light from the Sky

One night, Bunny hops into a field. She looks up at the sky. The stars sparkle. "I wish I had a star," says Bunny. Then something bright falls from the sky.

jhorrocks/E+/Getty Images

Bunny hops up to catch a falling star! "Time for bed," says Mama Bunny. So Bunny brings her star inside. Then she gets into bed. Her new night-light shines above her head.

Genre Study

 Talk about what makes Ellie's story a fantasy.

 Ask any questions you have about fantasy stories.

 Circle an event that could not really happen.

Plan

 Talk about a character for a fantasy story.

 Draw or **write** about the character and an event in your story.

Write the name of your fantasy character.

_____

- -

_____

Write about what your character does.

_____

- -

_____

- -

_____

- -

_____

Draft

Read Ellie's draft of her fantasy story.

Student Model

Night-Light from the Sky

One night, Bunny hops into a field. She looks up at the sky. The stars are pretty. "I wish I had a star," says Bunny. then something bright falls from the sky

Time Order
I put the events in order.

I wrote a complete sentence. It has a noun and a verb.

I used a picture dictionary to look up words I did not know how to spell.

Bunny hops up to catch a falling star! "Time for bed," says Mama Bunny. So Bunny brings her star inside. Then she gets into bed. Her new night-light shines above her head.

Writing Skill
I turned lines when I wrote.

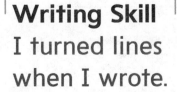
Your Turn

Begin to write your fantasy story in your writer's notebook. Use your ideas from pages 100-101.

Writing and Grammar

Revise and Edit

Think about how Ellie revised and edited her fantasy story.

I made sure to spell the word **_the_** correctly.

Student Model

Night-Light from the Sky

One night, Bunny hops into a field.

She looks up at the sky. The stars

sparkle. "I wish I had a star," says Bunny.

Then something bright falls from the sky.

I revised to use a more descriptive **verb**.

I edited this sentence. It begins with an uppercase letter and has an end mark.

Grammar

- A **verb** tells what someone or something is doing.
- **Prepositions** tell about nouns.

I added details to my picture.

Bunny hops up to catch a falling star! "Time for bed," says Mama Bunny. So Bunny brings her star inside. Then she gets into bed. Her new night-light shines above her head.

I checked that I used a **preposition** correctly in this sentence.

Your Turn

Revise and edit your fantasy story. Be sure to use verbs and sentences with prepositions. Use your checklist.

Share and Evaluate

 Practice presenting your work with a partner. Take turns.

 Present your work. Then use this checklist.

Review Your Work	Yes	No
Writing		
I wrote a fantasy story.	☐	☐
I wrote complete sentences.	☐	☐
I turned lines when I wrote.	☐	☐
Speaking and Listening		
I spoke in a loud, clear voice.	☐	☐
I answered questions using details.	☐	☐

Talk with a partner about your writing.

Write about your work.

What did you do well in your writing?

_____

- -

_____

_____

- -

_____

What do you need to work on?

_____

- -

_____

Time to Celebrate!

 Listen to "Our Country Celebrates!"

 Talk about national holidays in our country.

 Draw something people celebrate on one national holiday.

Talk about the reasons we celebrate national holidays.

Write one reason we celebrate these holidays.

_____

- -

_____

_____

- -

_____

Quick Tip

You can say:

We celebrate ____.

Holidays are important because ____.

Make a Holiday Postcard

 Talk about holidays that you celebrate.

What to Do

1. **Choose** a holiday that you celebrate.

2. **Draw** how you celebrate this holiday.

3. **Add** details.

4. **Write** a message to a friend about this holiday.

You Need

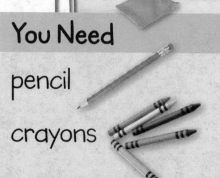

pencil

crayons

Choose Your Own Book

Minutes I Read

  Write the title of the book.

_____

- - - - - - - - - - - - - - - - - -

_____

  Tell a partner why you want to read it.
Then read the book.

  Write your opinion of the book.

_____

- - - - - - - - - - - - - - - - - -

_____

- - - - - - - - - - - - - - - - - -

_____

Think About Your Learning

Think about what you learned in this unit.

 Share one thing you did well.

 Write one thing you want to get better at.

_____

- -

_____

_____

- -

_____

Share a goal you have
with your partner.

My Sound-Spellings

Aa
a
apple

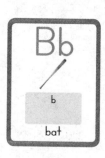
Bb
b
bat

Cc
c ck k
camel

Dd
d
dolphin

Ee
e
egg

Ff
f
fire

Gg
g
guitar

Hh
h_
hippo

Ii
i
insect

Jj
j
jump

Kk
c k ck
koala

Ll
l
lemon

Mm
m
map

Nn
n
nest

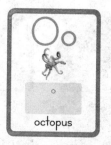
Oo
o
octopus

Pp
p
piano

Qq
qu_
queen

Rr
r
rose

Ss
s
sun

Tt
t
turtle

Uu
u
umbrella

Vv
v
volcano

Ww
w_
window

Xx
x
box

Yy
y_
yo-yo

Zz
z
_s
zipper

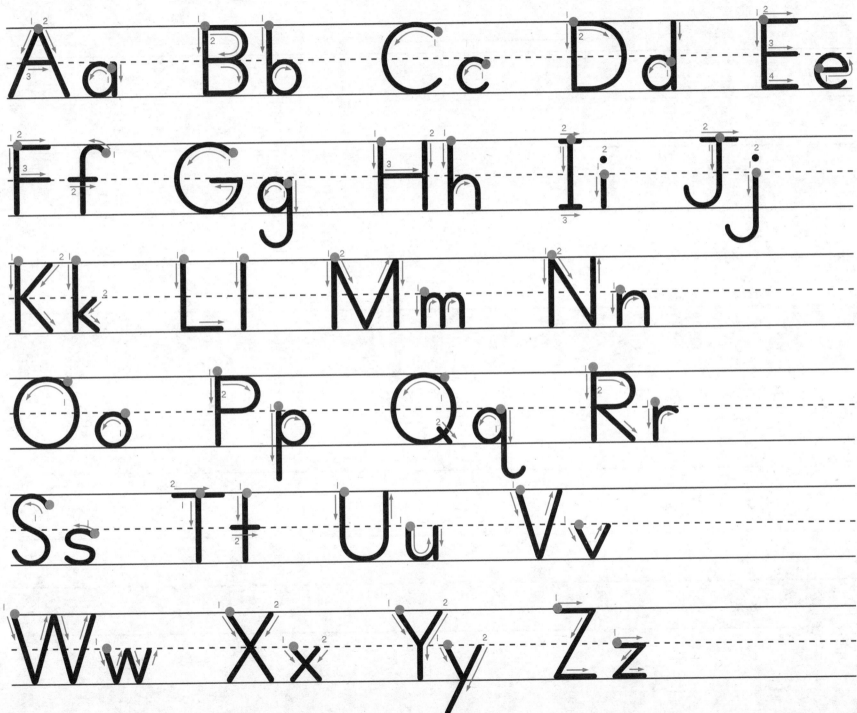